STARS IN THE MIND

MUSANJE PIUS

For the broken

ON BEING A POET

As the sky falls,

A poet sees not doom

But glory of the infinite;

The million suns and stars

Bowing low to kiss our hearts.

The poet tears his soul

Every sunrise and twilight,

And bleeds a metaphor or two

To bring life to all the unseen

Or buy happiness for men

To be a poet,

Is to fight peacefully

Against personal demons;

To be a poet,

Is to draw all feelings

And trade them for nothing

But a hope to rebirthing

Everything.

Table of Contents

BOOK ONE

A MAD MAN'S BIOGRAPHY

I

His hands competed with his head,

Each fighting to touch the gay earth

So both did glide upon the bed

At once, and came he out at birth

The wind, as cold as ice, hugged him

Before the nurse carried the frame

Of his body that seemed so slim,

Onto the weak but cheerful dame

She cried and smiled concurrently

At the lo sound of his first wail.

"Here lays my pain," she said bluntly,

As his silky skin turned but pale.

And as she left a day later,

She praised her hefty creator.

II

A name for him was suggested,

"Call him John like his late father,"

Repeated Grace; the beloved,

And the born baby's grandmother.

"His father died at a young age,

And was always drinking liquor,"

Reminded his mother with rage

And chose to name the boy Isaac.

He laughed, to fulfill the meaning,

And all welcomed the name given

But Jane disappeared complaining,

Soto voce, purely age driven.

The days became happier now

For he did bring a change somehow.

III

In his second year, he couldn't talk,

And his red gums buried most teeth;

His legs were to feeble to walk,

They were like a stem of wet heath.

His mother cried to the dumb gods

To speak a word or two for him

But even them couldn't shift the odds;

They had no wand to make him prim.

Time turned clouds into the blue sky

And the sly rains vanished away

From the region like a known spy

Who walks in shadows night and day.

At three, Isaac had grown too young:

Her mum's tit alone knew his tongue.

IV

The sad mother became worried

But neither did she dump her son

Nor label him a wasted seed

For she did desire still but non.

Indigenous herbs she did use

To mix and smear upon her tit

That Isaac may suck milk with nous

To spread sanity with each beat

Nothing did change the story flow;

He became a beast before men

But still his mum never let go,

She remained hoping now and then

But again fate darkened the days

With its surprising but vile rays.

V

The war between the mind and he

Befell the body with weight loss,

And thus too weak to lift his knee

Or flex, or move, or turn and toss.

The mother planted her weak boy

On her back like a bag of maize

Hoping a doc would treat her joy

And strike the allayed fire ablaze

"Your son dear woman, is insane,"

Cried the doc to the vexed parent

Who sorrowed in pain yet again

With non of help at the moment.

Rivers of tears bled from her eyes

Like dew raining before sunrise.

VI

His mother threw pity parties

To mourn her dead yet living son

For he was void of qualities

Having a worth under the sun

He grew too small and too fragile

Like a still stem in the desert,

Sun rays ablaze and sand hostile,

Knowing not the taste of comfort

All the leaves begin to wither

At such a young and bonnie age,

The wind continues to dither

With vapour, trying to assuage

But all the efforts fall in vain,

And also the sky makes no rain.

VII

On his seventh birthday, he cried;

He cried amidst hearty laughter,

A mixture of joyed and grieved eyes

For he knew not what comes after

Each one brought a gift and wishes,

And hugs that made him feel wanted

But their looks turned joy to ashes—

They were arrows from the gilded.

In the sane world he felt so lost;

Like earth is a place for the full

And not for they that have no cost—

The likely misplaced beasts who drool.

If he knew that heavens repair,

Perhaps he would ask in prayer.

VIII

As his mother slept by the wall,

Isaac sauntered out in silence—

Like the moon glowing after fall

When the day sees not the darkness

He threw a glance at the blank sky;

Such space for the lost and lonely!

Sirius, his fellow lone spy,

Was there to blink at him coyly.

His life painted his soul with grief

As he ambled down the dark path.

With the questions of a plucked leaf,

Unconscious of the aftermath.

He walked past all who knew his face

To a distant and unknown place.

IX

For hours he walked on the shadows

That lay as mats on the dry ground,

And souls accompanied him close

With scary songs of hellish sound.

Sunrise found him on the journey

With legs so tired and feet swollen.

His steps awoke birds so many,

And bees passed with bags of pollen.

All beings greeted the strange guest:

Dogs barked, thrashes chattered, cocks crowed,

And frogs croaked with voices so stressed;

Their vocal sacs 'bout to explode.

He, within a minute, gained fame

For all beasts longed to know his name.

X

His people searched in close cities

But non did find the missing child.

Posters were hanged on walls and trees,

Not knowing he'd become but wild.

"Oh God, don't take my only son,"

His sad mother cried day and night,

But fate had now made him a man;

He built his world with all his might.

A day bore weeks, and weeks bore months

Until it was years since the break.

His name got hidden in their mouths

But his mother earned a heartache.

Curses spiced her daily grievance

Until the words molded silence.

XI

Isaac grew in size and in age;

He was now as tall as a mast,

Pimples designed his smooth visage

And beards started to sprout so fast.

The soles of his feet were like stone—

He did not need a pair of shoes.

A thin cloth covered his crotch zone

When his clothes died with misuse.

His voice was thunder without rain,

That all turned whenever he yelled.

To they that stared, he barked again,

But among kids, he always dwelled.

He became an author of peace

But with actions of violence.

XII

The new world was free but lonely;

He went to all craved altitudes

But fellowshipped alone daily

E'en when he was in multitudes.

He made merry amidst mourning

And slapped a child that sought solace.

He raced with cars every morning

And knew folks at the marketplace.

The law rushed to the people's aid

And won the tough seizing battle

With an abrupt sedation raid

And left without any prattle.

In a health centre so lifeless,

Isaac joined those of his likeness.

XIII

Other patients, nude, welcomed him

With oceans of spit and laughter.

He was glad he'd got a new team

To go crazy with thereafter.

He bonded fast with everyone—

With both the staff and the patients;

They yapped and played from dawn to dawn

And his hobbies were arguments.

Days passed until Isaac got bored

Of the daily suchlike routines;

The injections, lectures, ill horde,

And the half-cooked posho and beans.

The days were chains of same events,

But Isaac had plans and intents.

XIV

He thought of ways out of that jail

And the primo was through disguise:

He attacked one nurse without fail

But had not thought about the size!

The dress was so tight for his frame

But withal, he marched to the gate,

His gait changed to that of a dame—

All features had to coordinate.

The gate was opened for the 'nurse',

And he walked out with his head high

No word came from the gatekeepers,

So he left without a goodbye.

He made merry in every form,

And basked in his newfound freedom.

XV

The sky sheltered his weary brain

And cooled it but with gusts of wind

For days and nights, in sun and rain,

As the dumpster met every need.

He smiled to the bright stars at night,

And Venus smiled back with a glow,

In search for him to make things right

But earth was far a place to know.

The skin on his body dried out

And patched firm onto his lean flesh

Like scales upon a healthy pout,

Its texture was defined with mesh.

Oh Isaac, that black crown you wear,

Is what defines pure need of care!

XVI

Life had nothing new to offer;

The sun rose and set the same way,

The heavy clouds still rained water,

But his life was now a highway.

His grown body now demanded

More than just daily food and drink.

The urge to function expanded

To an extent that he couldn't think.

As a fine dame passed by at night,

He tiptoed and grabbed her firmly.

Strength was the fuel for his sleight;

His hands wrapped the lone dame tightly.

He drowned in a sea of pleasure

By stealing the woman's treasure.

XVII

The sun arrived and shone madly

As Isaac snored near the woman

That drew attention of many

Who asked about the sleeping man.

She cried and told the whole event,

And each word was a piece of wood

That stirred their fire to an extent

That all were put in the worst mood.

They beat Isaac in the worst way

With bare punches, kicks, stones and canes

'Til life started to bleed away

Through gushes of blood from his veins.

He stayed at the mercy of fate

But no one seemed to care as yet.

XVIII

He whined in pain, blood-soaked wholly,

For the sun and houseflies to treat;

For none did try to act holy,

So there he lay—just on the street.

The awful day crawled to evening

But none cared for the dying man.

His weak vision was now blurring

While dusk foretold his short lifespan.

As his soul was bidding farewell,

Isaac uttered a blaring cry,

Perhaps trying to break the bad spell

But death was never his ally.

His cry disappeared in midair

And death captured him unaware.

XIX

His mother felt a sharp dagger

Navigate through her broken heart

As she walked out with a stagger,

From her dark hut, into the night,

As though she'd heard Isaac's last call.

She replied with rivers of tears;

Of both her lost son's unknown fall

And the cancer that brought her fears.

She saw the moon behind a fold

Of the dense clouds, hiding its face,

And felt her son's body grow cold,

Far from her warm arms—its safe place.

Her knees trembled as she went back

To mourn her gone son in the dark

XX

She lay upon the weeping bed

In tears of death and a son lost;

The part of her, gone at the end,

With non of concern but her ghost.

She crawled from her body below

And left it cold for soil and worms

That danced inside the aged barrow

Where her mate lay with open arms

Welcoming his love for wedlock

But in the darkness of the grave

Where all is bound into deadlock

And breath is for insects to crave.

Her corpse was buried with a tear

For Isaac's cry she could not hear.

BREATH OF LIFE

Weak lungs dance

At the taste of you;

Their envelops unwind

And read love letters

To the lonely heart,

Which smiles with red petals

Into sad streams of blood.

The magic creates a pace

For frozen bodies.

CHAMBERS IN THE SKY

In an enormous world, an insect flies.

Its belly is an afterlife for various lives

And its head, a home for many aces.

On its back, it carries a heavy chamber;

A space that holds the world it lives in.

With pride it flies, aiming for the top.

The load on its back is a sea of sweat,

Waiting for a single stare to burst

Into a new world which the insect rules:

Where the sky is not the limit

And the stares are but praises of those

That used to laugh at its broken wings.

A chamber in the sky is all one needs

To create a new world void of sweat.

As our foes study the stages of our lives,

The angels sing to guide our little hope

Until we grow to fill the spaces above us

With the creatures we have in our minds.

FATHER

In his weary pages,

A father holds the words

That make up your soft life.

The handwriting is poor;

Each text a punishment

For his love and goodness.

All letters tear his joy

In order to complete

The long story of you.

Destruction will meet him

After bearing so long

Each syllable and foot.

But before he decays,

Teach, fix and entertain

He who dares to read you.

FALL ON ME

Fall on me, dear sky;

Fall down and fill me

As I walk up these stairs

To reach your endless top,

Make the stars my eyes

And the woolen clouds,

The skin to cover my bones.

Let the cinnabar rays of sunset

Blind all the endless worries

That lay in my ancient soul.

Fall on me, dear heavens

And make gods of gift buds

Like the glided orchid seeds

That hang bonny blooms

With kisses of rain and time.

Let your winds lift my arms

To touch the invisible and,—

And the ghostly figures

That form shadows

That color the night.

GONE DAYS

Eroded by the flow of time

And diminished by the new,

Old days harbor in memories

Behind, in trapped pieces of me

Sheltered, but forbidden to roam

Imprisoned without a crime,

Perhaps some events so blue

That shambled past boundaries

But now on bare knees with plea;

In savage hopes, trying to get home

Past and present never rhyme

But without past, we've no value

So we should bury all the worries

And let the happier days break free

From the forget-the-history syndrome

We have but a deficient lifetime

And loved ones who stay are few

Quit all beauty stains in mysteries

That draw a future that will never be

Believe me, hark to this subtle gnome.

MY ASCENSION

Darkness

Bound my eyes

With fears and grime

For my heart to run cold,

Pumping still quivers

Into these veins

But I need healing,

A light that will shine for me

To unveil each fold of death,

A salvation from desolation,

An overflow of existence

Even when what surrounds me

Is a pack of limitations.

Divine wings I long for

To hype me from the silence

And tight chains of my dinky world.

Let my sight crawl above the soil

That blankets me underneath,

To see the light on the sky

And the limitless world

To strive for the clouds

And milk every drop

That was created

For my delight

Before time.

THE JOURNEY

Every step blinds the way:

That is how the song goes

From those life threw away,

To us who live with woes

Earth is mellow no more

And gold has become stone.

Cheating for perfect score

Has made victims to moan.

Life moves by the music

You give while hot or cold:

Plant deeds so angelic

And shut smiles will unfold

'We shall start tomorrow'

Is a dangerous thought,—

God's wand we can't borrow

To book the next day's slot

Seasons change quarterly,

Each dose of sun and rain;

A chance to make merry,

Lest your sweat drip in vain

Learn from every mistake,

And if God gives you wings,

Fly and conquer and take,

But don't bear greed like pigs.

THE STAND

Sermon inequality and racism–

The two beasts living in the herd,

That the lambs have grown into lions,

Overnight; fill the burrows to the brim

For there's nothing left to hide in them.

Watch the spears align their fingers

As fine swords erect in their gums

The ashes that built the ground

Converge at the terminal in merry,

To the accomplishment of the cause

And the rebirth of ancient supremacy;

The giant footprints that faded unseen,

Yet directed multitudes of brave men

To journey through thicker woods.

Let the blind man wipe his eyes

With decayed stains of black blood

That toiled for ages amidst no tidings;

Before this world up rose from iniquity.

Watch the dark moon replace the sun,

As the day dies and masses scatter

To the ending which fate assured.

THE TRANSITION

Fate and destiny are subtle

But if life be my grave

Then mortality is my mantle

That makes me brave

Retired are the arms that bore me

And my past is present no more

Now home is no longer a place to be

For a man ought to rise up and go

Farewell to my dear youthful days

For you have taught me a lot

But I am the future ready to amaze

They that see me as a sunspot

Let hope therefore be my companion

As love mentors me with pride

To build my legacy against any oblivion

That tries to mount on my side

BOOK TWO

BREAKUP ANNIVERSARY

Uplift my weak spirit yet again,

For these wounds still hurt like then

When you crossed the river without me

As I got visions of us but failed to foresee

That your approval would become profane.

Break me twice but never push me away,

Adorn each sorrow with perfect sense

And forsake me not into this loneliness,

Uplift my weak spirit yet again!

Let my gaze jump over those walls

To see you again clear like new bronze

As you renew me with your perpetual love

That died at a time not different to this

But I've never learnt to let go with such ease:

Uplift my weak spirit yet again!

BROKEN CREED

In writings, I drown you unfeigned

And put you before innocent souls

Which share my pain, to forbid my end

But I bury you in the depth of my heart,

Where you rise with faded moments

To grasp traces of air for me to breathe

Life oozes out of me as I recite you;

Each gust I spit to utter your name

Cuts my throat with desperate groans

But my lips soak in the sweetness of it,

Knowing that you still exist within me

To add warmth inside my stale memory

BUDS OF SORROW

I thought fate was clear

When it separated us, my dear

But memories in my head

And moments never made

Give me no reason to spare

The fact that you don't care

I can't reach you now—

Yes, I can, but don't know how

That silence has left my world in pain,

My unending efforts you've seen in vain.

I'm still waiting for new love to spark,

But alas, my world seems forever dark.

CROWN ME

Crown me, dear one,

With your love I long for.

Search my heart for any hope

To bring down that raised tower

That stands against you and I.

Let's give room to reunion

And forsake sad history

Crown me, evil one,

With that crown of thorns,

Make my blood drip invisibly

Into this pen and onto this paper.

Strike with your wand again

And nail me down to dust,

Reveal every mystery.

DEAD WORSHIP

I stood in the cold to evoke the spirit of you,

In the dark, my clothes shone a little more

The adoration lasted but without your clue

And none of the prayers crossed that door

Beneath my melted skin was a set sacrifice

Ready to cleanse and renew your proud love

But your shrewd heart grew colder than ice

Nothing melted it, not even the sun above

My weak legs could not bear your fairness

So I ceded to your will to the least of time

But before me you put a mighty fortress

And saving me was a dead tale in a mime

I always wish you'd rekindle the days of old

But the fact remains that you are not God

DREAMS

Dressed in series of persistent pain

My mind clings to non but you again

A dead memory is reborn timely as I lay

To drain my tears 'til crying can't portray

That it's you I see in every windowpane

Your smile strikes my ego like a hurricane

And teaches my heart never to restrain

With resilient forms, but to always obey

Even in series of persistent pain.

I can't awaken from each dream or abstain

From the feelings that they always contain.

Come again and make your presence stay

Drift my mind far from this reality, away

From my clouded eyes yet to pour out rain

With series of persistent pain.

HAPPY HEARTBREAK!

Boxing Day was an hour old

So young that it hadn't known

The taste of the morning sun

Or tears from the crying skies

So determined, as all made merry,

She never knew boundaries of life.

My heart became the victim of fate

That knocked to cause rampage.

With an honor of writing to me,

She scribbled down a piece of hell,

Ready to devour my soul entirely

Without hearing her seraphic voice.

Emptiness filled my dumbstruck spirit,

As oceans maneuvered from my eyes.

With the fading sound of the jingle bells,

She wished me a happy heartbreak!

INTERNAL BATTLES

Lonely chaos spreads like a fire

In the depth of my heart;

Like an erupting desire

Tearing my mind and soul apart

Underneath it is a forlorn choir

That suffocates any restart

With choruses of satire

That leave doors to her not shut

LOVE AT FIRST SIGHT

The first and second so clueless

Like a timid flower 'bout to see a bee,

I sprang, in the third with freshness

At the sight of what seemed to be

The beginning of my eternal dream

Coated with such breath of reality.

Ridges across that smooth neck,

Bore all streams the world has never held

Like tides on an enormous ocean,

I shook, time and forth to hallucinations

Into a world with nature's finest gift

To me, the least of the undeserving

Pieces of me I wrote to the erupting fount

For a wish or two into Marigold fields;

From a lower altitude to peaks of more

Like the uplifting spirit in falling rain,

You possessed me and bid farewell

To the self in me who froze with the cold

LOVE LETTER I

My mind glitters

With dreams about you

Like the silent rising

Of a formidable prayer

That ends a fire incarnate,

The sparks you ignite in me

Terpsichore with a rhythm

Revealed by the breaking of

The masculine latch in me.

Swaying in a fine melody

Is my restless heart

To the warmth you give

Unfolding the knots at each vein

Making fountains of blood

That invisibly color

My trepid consciousness

At the sight of you.

LOVE LETTER II

God drew your beauty

On the ceiling of the earth

For dusk to feed on

Whenever you fade with sleep

And my mind dreams not of you.

LOVE LETTER III

The weight in my heart

Is depicted by the tears

That bleed from my eyes

When you appear in dreams

And yet your beautiful face

Is never seen at daybreak

The darkness infested

From the night to daytime

Comes with flashes of you

From my wildest dreams,

Laughing at the efforts I put

In trying to escape the past.

LOVE LETTER IV

Can we meet tonight?

Inside the dreams in my head,

Or those that dwell in yours?—

In the shadows of the night;

Untroubled by the reality,

Revisiting memories.

I'm at the back of your mind

Where fate confirms not

That our story lost its breath

And that I'm not welcome

To orchestrate your pleasure

Meet me behind twilight

Where the day peeps not at us

And the dark night lives

But on the outside of you.

LOVE LETTER V

I wish to see the stars glow

But their beauty can't fix me,

So I choose to close my eyes

That my mind may fancy you.

If I could dream forever,

I would build a world for us;

Far from the real chains of life

As tears wash the pain away.

Endless fears lie in my soul:

Fears that I have to wake up

And yet you vanish at dawn

With the silent death of Nox.

LOVE LETTER VI

The dark sky is weeping,

As Venus tries to dry his tears;

Because you, the brightest of all,

Glided your rays through thin air

And disappeared with the sun.

If the moon was winged,

Or gifted with words like mine,

It would steal you from my dreams

And offer your face to the sky

When midnight darkness arrives

But I guard you jealously

For I own only the delicate pieces

Which I broke from your soul

Before the rest of you drowned

In reality; my greatest enemy.

LOVE LETTER VII

The freshness of the heavens

Falls down in the night

To cover my skin and bones

As a suit for the reunion

With you, their own.

The stars make a standing ovation

For your soul as it rallies

With tidings from the old days

To make it to my dreams

LOVE LETTER VIII

I stand frozen in this cold,

Like a naked bird by the shore;

My mind rains of smiles of you,

Waiting for the pale moon to strike

Its dull rays onto my eyes—

A dose of absolute hypnosis.

The distance across the sky dies,

I cling to one red dwarf star;

It is the flower I bring you tonight,

Those opaline eyes don't need the sun.

Reach for my hand, dream guest,

And pray we get trapped here

Forever, with the world in my mind

And time not on our wrists.

Let your smiles drool of memories

As my dreams make them come true.

LOVE LETTER IX

We conquered the whole universe

And lit it up with fervent kisses

That sparkle when our lips meet;

Our creations give taste to the world

All the lovely dreams we shared

Became secret but written realms

Visited by those that saw us not;

All people bow when our eyes meet

I saw the sun imitate your smile,

Hoping the moon would write about her

Like I do when you bloom in my mind;

The petals you bear color my sky.

Before the sun envies our love

And interrupts us with its rising,

Let my heart beat one more time;

I live, but only in dreams with you.

LOVE LETTER X

After these sly dreams,

I fall into faded hopes

That my hand meets yours.

MARIA

You bore the curse

Of open arms from all,

Sweet blossomed flower.

Can I just water you

With my words so fine

To lick your lovely petals?

My life bleeds darkness,

Your world shines so bright.

Maria, can I be your shelter?

Serenity turns to anguish

At the sound of the fact that

My warmth is too cold for you.

MIDNIGHT CRY

I'm the sky above

Diseased with so much space

But my stars dance

To the beat in your heart

Beckon me, once again

And drive the night away

From my lonely chambers

NOSTALGIA

Still stuck in the day's porch,

I looked in my spirit and saw

The broken part of me like so

On my knees begging for mercy

With tears that rolled into a sea

In which my words sank in depth

With zilch left under this scorch,

I stand on my feet with great awe

Don't tell me you hadn't any flaw—

For the dark me is all you could see.

I never got warnings from banshee

For you buried me before my death

Still longing for your gentle touch

That tamed my senses ne'er to abhor,

Rather raise this whim more and more

To crave for the impossible to a degree

Of non but me becoming your devotee,

Whose content will rise at loss of breath.

OUR SKY

I did try

To count the stars;

Tens of hundreds,

Of thousands of them

In the sky

We shared

But I didn't realize

It was just as far as

My eyes could go.

I missed seeing

The millions

Beyond.

RESURGENCE

The broken past lingers timely

In confound memories of her

But longs to be reborn each day

With specks of love and pain

SEA OF BITTERNESS

Sea of bitterness

I feel you flood inside my chest

Drown me no more

For I've already met the Grim reaper

Spit me to the shore

And let your fingers wet me in the day

Sea of bitterness

You pierce my skin with your chilly pins

Spare my last breath

Embrace me gently, don't break my bones

Notice my warm tears

And separate them from your frozen waters

Sea of bitterness,

How I long to swim in your deep dark ends!

THE FALL OF US

The sky was stained with darkness

And only its perforations aided my eyes;

Perforations that grew smaller but brighter,

To imagine the light beyond my sight

So vivid but out of reach

Tears broke out with my crushed heart

Through my eyes like melted streams

Across a block of ice; their mother,

Into nothingness

My mind was shot dumb

As the whole world succumbed

To the cause of the fall of us.

THE MARTYRED SOUL

Set before a cruel judge and minors,

A siren, last of its kind, was sounded.

He was judged first of other offenders

Innocent or guilty, he would be beheaded.

The past and the future pleaded for him

But the judge's face was tinted with grim

Blisters of agony eroded his youthful jest

As all odds stained his name to their best

"Pillars of hope, fortify, don't let me fall"

His muffled voice betrayed him with haste

For fate minds not about faith after all.

Pilgrims he'd made for her met hardliners

Whose acts of torture are still unfounded.

Dipped in boiling pain for some answers,

He felt tangled but as hairs were abducted,

A stream of bitter words drowned his whim

For they didn't know prices of being a victim

Not even one had suffered a mere arrest

Only the heavens knew how this did taste

Hours later, as the judge made the last call,

Alibi sacrificed wholly but went unaddressed

For fate minds not about faith after all.

As all reasoned out in their small clusters,

The voices made an unclear song accorded

Of friends and family, but they, the accusers,

Shouted in agreement for the moment awaited

As shots of anger tore his mind in the prelim.

While the devil's choir sang the last hymn,

Guilt was present to have him confessed

About selfless deeds that had him messed

Without revealing what calamity would befall

When a spear was struck first to his chest

For fate minds not about faith after all

Too far from any of his secret altars,

Darkness that filled him was abounded

So it allied with despair to be afterburners

Hopes rose no more from being grounded

As the fires of happiness became dim,

Memories appeared a little clearer to skim

Any joy and laughter that tried to congest

All the promises for him were undressed

As smiles of disbelief formed a waterfall

But non could rise for him in protest

For fate minds not about faith after all

He is the greatest among all headliners

Vulnerable he lay when he was confounded

Signaling to they who want to be imitators,

That true love will by no means be accepted

However sweet and sanctified it may seem

Because its power burnt and buried his vim

No tear maneuvered down unexpressed

But the pain born can never be suppressed

Agony burns his throat like shots of alcohol

On fire, like soldiers on their way to a quest

For fate minds not about faith after all.

Truly love hearkens not to any guest

Even when you have something to suggest,

It will drown you in incognito as a whole

And inevitably make you its conquest

For fate minds not about faith after all

UNANSWERED PRAYERS

As the baby raindrops

Break through with ease

The multitudinous layers

Of the atmosphere

To kiss the alien ground,

So does my love strive

To burst out of my obscure heart,

Longing to paint your mind

With memories and dreams,

And possibilities we have

When we give one final beat

To the Lazarus of our tale.

BOOK THREE

19:16

Underneath this dome of darkness,

The cry of light is unheard;

Deafened by the stroll of invisibility

To temporary eternal rest

Fulfill the prophesy, divine blindness

And give sight to the night

For your soul has yielded with glory

And the sun-god has lost

A CITY NIGHT: THE LIGHTS

Those stars that glitter

On tombs of the undead

Are the ever-open eyes

That look into the night

To cast out the spell

Of darkness.

They mimic galaxies above,

Shout of various colors

And seek the secrets

That hide in corners

Of the dark side.

How glorious it is

To rest sleepy eyes

Upon those glary holes

That vomit rays in midair

To stretch living shadows!

AFTER THE RAIN

After bidding farewell to the rains,

The mud scatters into pieces of dust

Birthing grippe; burying malaria banes,

Floods and existence of metal rust.

The sun falls down and ripens grains,

And the grown legume pods burst.

A fagged leaf breaks off from a tree,

Sinks in mid air, worshipping the sun

As milky blood drips from the amputee

To cast a spell of death to its lost son;

When the latter thinks it's now 'free',

The soil bathes it and they become one.

The empty sky sings of sole wonder

With its blue sea soaked in fiery rays,

Silent, void of lightning and thunder;

Rather the sight of birds as they praise,

In unknown tongues, the view under—

A created beauty of inexplicable ways.

BLUE SKY

My sight sinks deep into you,

Fishing the flying lands afar;

I ran out of space in my mind

To search the space you bear.

Sometimes I call you an ocean

But your waves riot in stillness

And your boundaries can never

Be defined by my pinhole eyes.

Your eye is as bright as a fire,

I cannot stare into it and read

What your invisible brain holds,

Or the plans hidden at its back.

Oh blue sky: the undrawn map

Of the unknown lost creations;

The holder of concealed realms,

How I long to delimit your roots!

CLOUDY

Darkness whispers now

As gloomy clouds fill the sky;

Night falls during day.

DARKENED SKY

As the bats watch you;

'So deep' is their expression,

Hanging upside down.

DEAR EVENING SUN

Dear evening sun,

It's been many seasons now

Since you made all of me bow

To your then dying face

The last flickering hope

Wandered about to each peak

Before your rays became weak

In silent battles

Multitudes of tears

Race from the sky above

Trying to make you groove

Across the horizon

Impossibly

DUSK AND DAWN

After the day grows weary,

The sun sleeps and waits

For the next morning's crown,

When darkness creeps out

And the empty sky unmasks

Its endless blue chambers

FULL MOON

Blind hole drawn on the sky

Stare at me with modesty

Like I'm the missing wolf

That fellowships with you

On a night that's not tonight

MORNING

As this new day breaks,

I wake up from my nightmares

To see the sun smile

RAIN

Transient patches you paint

On my battered skin so faint

Cure my injured soul instantly

With quivers stabbing decently

Through your gelid droplets,

Father and I dance like mates

To the beat of the uniform rant,

Like two youth dogs after a hunt

Glorious are the days so cold

With the sky as the threshold

To your invisible naked mother

Whose children are like no other

The sun needs a better half

To rule the day on its behalf.

Clouds are empty without you,

Fill them and make the sky new.

RAIN-KISSED

The stinging rain drops

Fall onto my broken skin

And lodge chills in me

RESTART

My windowpane glows;

A fresh beginning signals

Light on a new day.

OWLS

With black moons for eyes,

Owls stare blindly in the dark

To halt beating hearts.

BOOK FOUR

14/04/1865

His sight lost in a play.... A silly play,

Of laughter that ironically mourns

And many faces that are lower

And yet won't look up to him.

See, another play begins—

A play of one, a play that's not a play

A play that ends in history, sad history,

Where people, like children in rain,

Go helter-skelter with the blast;

The sound of the final curtain.

18/05/1965

I witnessed Venus tumble

And compress the hearts of all.

Legacy seeped life out of him

As he left the sky bare and dark

His warm body grew frigid

With a wipe of the southern wind

And the sharp eyes of many

That pierced his skin with stares

He can never be seen again;

The devoted light lost its clarity

To the enemy of his universe

But shines forever, yet concealed!

A DAILY FAREWELL

The butterflies my aunt sent me

Are black and grey.

They do fly,

Around the light in my eyes,

And scary dreams they do bring

As I accompany silent souls

Through a notion of loneliness;

The millions of seconds in the night.

The sky disappears

And the darkness solidifies

Into rooms with undefined ends

But small enough to warm my smile

I stretch my arms to touch her hidden face:

I feel it...

It's like the first sight of daylight,

The smoothness of a new sun.

She kneels on the still air

And sends the wind to hug me

For her hands are too feeble

To grasp the life in my body

She jokes but without a smile,

"Your scars became shadows of me,"

The words I poured in her ears disappear;

Her eardrums make their own beat,

And all words from me now are but written:

She forgot how to read and write!

But nevertheless,

With her cold heart in my hands,

I say to her in the softest voice,

"I miss the sound of your heartbeat."

DEATH ON TRIAL

Whisper to me, oh selfish death:

Does your belly stretch to the sea?

Is your gut a foeman of breath?

Don't explain something I can't see!

For long you've spread your arms so wide

Across all things, seen and unseen—

Sinless or guilty, none can hide

From the cold you shelter therein.

All the witnesses have arrived;

Orphans, widows and vilomahs,

And all whose people ever lived,

Come with evidence of their scars.

The pains you water down their hearts,

Have nurtured the wrath they owe you.

I won't wait to hear all their stats:

You have been sentenced to death too!

LETTER TO THE DEAD

These truths that fall in your cold ears

Are drops of tears drained from my heart;

Warm and red, like these many years

Since you and us were split apart.

We mourn and cry to fate and time,

And pray to God but in silence,

Sometimes we cry with song and rhyme

To drain the pains of your absence.

Even without your sole effect,

The world's features are still the same:

Rocks and mountains still stand erect,

And the sun never lost its flame.

We hope the grave isn't a prison

Like this binding life you left us—

It mistreats us with no reason,

But death's call too makes us anxious.

Soon we will make merry again

When our breath departs our lungs too,

But til then, we'll ache with the pain

Which, with your presence afar, grew.

SUNSET SONG

As I inevitably die this slow,

Forget not to pray for my light

For I will rise again but not to all;

Some will have met their end

My luminance is all I show

To darkness that plants fright

In you and that makes you crawl;

Begging the moon to transcend

As my body goes down below,

Let the stars shine in your night

And hope your oblivion doesn't fall

At your feet until I finally ascend.

THE LOSS

On that cold day,

I lost you on the wings of rain

Too weak to lift both of us

I thought I could leave you to fly

But gravity always pulled you down

And into the ground you disappeared

Like love in the hearts of men

THE WIDOW

The widow by the cold river bank

Is not a day dreamer

But sits on her brown mat daily

Calling the man he sees stand

On the still water

The lonely widow meditating

Isn't a philosopher.

She's just a believer praying

That fate unites her spirit

With her husband's soul

The weeping widow in the dark night

Isn't her self anymore;

She lost her other better half

To the mysterious grave

Before their love broke.

TOMB FOR THE BROKEN

Walking through catacombs

Of this lonely tomb

Mysteries untold, unveiled

With ferries of fear

Scars scratched by dirt of old

As cobwebs lay void

Insight of an eternal bed

Than soak my blood

Held captive in this darkness

Yet my mind blossoms

With memories of the light

In confined jests

Beneath your idempotent words

Mornings are unheeded

The light is buried in darkness

And sopor conquers

YOURS, THE BURIED

My body hurts

I'm clothed in numbness

I need to flex, I need to turn;

To walk, to run, to dance,

And, perhaps,

To feel the smooth fingers of life–

The few minutes of endless joy

In my darling's embrace,

Like the heavy clouds on a wet sky,

Masturbating each other for pleasure;

The downpour of rain...

But my house is too small and dark,

Too small to harbor

My wife and my spirit

And too dark to recognize anyone I know...

My eyes and jaws ache

My skin bleeds cold sweat

I feel hollow, my worms are dead

I need to feed them back to life.

It's been a while since I last had a bath

My suit and stockings need a wash too.

I'm already tired of sleeping,

Infinite sleep without dreams is an infection

Which has eaten all but my bones

And has made my house crowd with stink.

Oh, I miss the pellucid mornings

And pitch nights with golden seals,

Along with the music of the nightingales,

Those lonely birds that appear not

When the night is full of gales.

Which year is it?

It's as if I've spent a decade here

And yet you visit me not.

I always talk to myself

I think I'm running mad,

I can't feel my lips move as I speak.

Please tell me I'm alright,

Do you hear me when I cry?

RSVP